Werewolf
Granny

Werewolf Granny

Poems about Families

Selected by
TONY BRADMAN

Illustrated by
Colin Paine

BLOOMSBURY
CHILDREN'S
BOOKS

For Molly and Frank – C.P.

First published in Great Britain in 1999
Bloomsbury Publishing Plc, 38 Soho Square, London, W1V 5DF

Individual poem details feature on the acknowledgements
page located at the back of this book
Copyright © Text this selection Tony Bradman 1999
Copyright © Illustrations Colin Paine 1999

The moral right of the author has been asserted
A CIP catalogue record of this book is available from the
British Library

ISBN 0 7475 4486 7

Printed in England by Clays Ltd, St Ives plc

10 9 8 7 6 5 4 3 2

Contents

Aunties Galore

Have I got aunties? I've got stacks of 'em –
heaps and hordes and piles and packs of 'em.
An abundance of aunties swarming round
like ants
they make me jerseys, scarves, socks . . .
and knitted underpants.
Everywhere I look there's an auntie sitting
an auntie telling stories,
nattering and knitting.
There are aunts in every cupboard,
aunties under the stairs,
aunties under the table,
aunts in all the chairs,
aunties watching telly,
aunties drinking tea,
aunties on the sofa . . .

and no room left for me.

Michaela Morgan

David

I should have been David,
the son they so wanted,
they had his name ready,
they had the blue gear
and two older sisters
to look after him here.
But fate double-crossed them
and I came along –
as his little imposter
I knew I was wrong.

If, as I think,
the unborn have ghosts,
then David's the one
who haunts me most.
He borrows my thoughts,
he calls me a phoney,
says that it's he
should be here,
he'd come into his own
if I'd disappear.

But over the years
we've come to agree
that I'm as much David
as David is me.
He the dream child,
I the one born,
but sharing together
that gossamer space,
where dream and reality
meet and join.

Diana Hendry

Driving at Night with My Dad

Open the window,
the cool summer night swooshes in.
My favourite cassette playing loud.

2am – summer's midnight –
neither of us can sleep
so we go for a night drive.

Stars crowd the sky
and twinkle at us in code.
Our headlights reply in light language.

A fox crosses, red and grey,
and arches under a fence:
rabbits run and a farm cat's eyes
catch our beam.
She stares at us for a second of stretched
    time . . .
. . . her eyes two new coins.

Through villages that are asleep,
past farms that are warm,
past houses that are dreaming,
under trees that are resting,
past birds that have no flight, no song.

I sense I am in some other country
where day, time, people no longer matter.
In this huge dark,
through the somewhere and the nowhere
of this uninhabited world,
I feel safe and secure
driving at night with my dad.

John Rice

Parentspeak

If I've told you
A thousand times
I've told you once
Don't gobble your food
Think yourself lucky
There are people starving
How often must I tell you
Mark my words
Don't slam that door
Isn't it time you were asleep
Why won't you ever
Get out of bed?
What was that you said?

Why must you argue?
Children should
Be seen and not heard
When I was your age
I wouldn't have dared
There's no such
thing as can't
I can't believe what
I'm hearing

Don't say 'ain't' or 'innit'
I'll give you your
Pocket money
In a minute, in a minute

Have you done
Your homework?
I haven't got a clue
You shouldn't be listening
It's got nothing
To do with you
You don't own the
Television, I pay the bills
What did your last
Servant die of?
Come on, we haven't
Got all year . . . I've told
You a thousand times
It'll all end in tears . . .

Tony Bradman

Divorce

It's not **you** that I'm leaving.

You know that Mum and Dad don't
get on very well any more, and
I've just had enough.

No, we don't love each other now.
Yes, we used to. Well,
I think we did.
No, of course it's not our fault.
It's nobody's fault really. It's just that
your mum won't listen.

She says that about me?

You know we both love you.
You'll be all right with Mum, and
I'll see you
every Sunday.

Don't forget
it's not **you** that I'm leaving

not **you** that I'm leaving

you that I'm leaving

I'm leaving.

Mike Jubb

Just Mine

This was my brother's jumper.
You can see it doesn't fit.
It makes me look all floppy.
And I feel a twit.

These were my sister's blue jeans.
They're long and loose and baggy.
They make it hard to walk along.
And my legs look saggy.

But these are my brand new shiny boots.
And they fit just fine.
I can walk in them the way I want.
They're MINE!

Tony Mitton

Listening in Bed

If I listen hard
in bed at night,

I can hear
the floor creak,
the door squeak,
the tap leak.

I can hear
the dishes clink
down in the kitchen sink.

I can hear
the telly boom
down in the sitting room.

And very near
I can hear
my little brother
breathing deep.
Sssssh . . .
He's fast asleep.

Tony Mitton

Family Laughs

I laugh like a machine gun,
My brother laughs like a truck,
My sister laughs like a turkey,
My auntie laughs like a duck.

Grandad laughs like a thunderstorm,
My mother laughs like a clown,
But my father's laugh
is the weirdest of all:
It's like a balloon going down.

Eric Finney

Sisterly Love

That's my cushion,
I had it first.
Mum made me clean my room
But yours is worse.

That's my yo-yo.
That's my pen.
You took my Barbie.
You broke my Ken.

You squashed my doughnut.
You ate my cake.
You nicked the stickers
I swopped at break.

Don't come near me.
Don't breathe my air.
Now Mum's telling *me* off –
THAT'S NOT FAIR!

Judy Waite

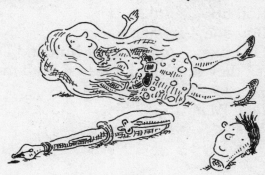

This Week's Bargain Boys

Roll up,
Roll up,
Get your Brothers here.
I've got one going cheap
With just a small flea in his ear.

Roll up,
Roll up,
Hurry while stocks last.
This one's free with every soap –
Oh – please don't hurry past!

Roll up,
Roll up,
They come complete with toys
And slugs and mud and bits of gum
And bags of healthy noise.

Roll up,
Roll up,
Buy one – get one free.
Oh crikey – here come Mum and Dad
. . . they don't look pleased with me . . .

Judy Waite

Me

According to
My family
I have:

Dad's nose
Mum's eyes
Uncle Bob's mouth
Auntie Jean's chin
Grandpa's legs
Granny's hair
Sister Lucy's hands
Brother Paul's feet
And Cousin Sally's knees

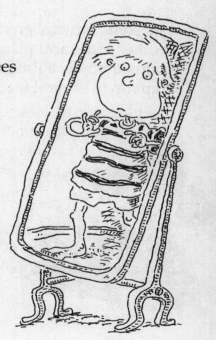

But no one
Can explain why
I have this
Peculiar feeling
Constantly

This feeling
Of being

Me

Tony Bradman

Grandma's Funeral

The funeral done, I watched them come,
In small groups, walking slow;
In solemn black, they all trudged back,
Heads down and talking low.

But when they'd had their sandwiches,
And cakes and cups of tea,
Once they began to talk of Gran,
It seemed to set them free.

And some remembered tales of her
In other times and places;
And in a while, a little smile
Crept on to several faces.

And then the smiles turned into grins,
And chuckles followed after,
Her sense of fun, the things she'd done,
Soon had them filled with laughter.

She wouldn't mind, for should I write
My grandma's epitaph,
I'd make it clear – *my gran lies here*
Who always loved a laugh.

Barry On

Walking Home with My Foster Father
(December 1948)

My hand in his and both inside his pocket.
Six years old and out at night, walking home.
Frost haloes ringed each street-lamp
Round rainbows of yellow-green.
Cold air rasped my lungs.
Pavements glittered ice.

Our boots left hot black prints in white rime.
My toes would not separate.
The moon puffed cloud vapour across stars.
The world seemed bigger with its blue peeled
    back.
He'd told me once, 'Out there . . . that's
    Space.'
Rough tweed scratched my wrist.

His hand was very warm.
The smell of sawn logs seeped from his
  overalls.
'Look, there's The Plough,' he said,
'And there's The Giant.'
A giant farming the sky, I thought
And stared at the fields of space.

Catherine Benson

Swinging

Push me, Mummy, push me
High up in the air,
Higher, Mummy, higher,
Send me over there

Where that branch is growing,
This is so much fun!
Let me touch those leaves, Mummy,
Let me touch the sun.

Swing me, Mummy, swing me,
Do you call this high?
Let me touch that house there, Mummy,
Let me touch the sky.

Stop me, Mummy, stop me,
Get me off this swing!
My ears are starting to pop, Mummy,
My head is starting to ring.

Oh, the ground is spinning!
I think I'm going to die.
Really, Mummy, why did you
Push the swing so high?

Valerie Bloom

Sisters

We're sisters, me and Clare.
I'm dark, she's fair.
She's the taller, she's the bolder,
Always rushing. Two years older.

Throw a ball, Clare will catch it,
Read a book, Clare will snatch it,
Got a secret, Clare will shout it,
All the world will know about it.

When I say please, she says no.
She yells at me because I'm slow.
She can't bear to wait a minute.
Every game, she has to win it.

I like to read, she likes rough games,
I call my mum, she calls me names.
People say we're chalk and cheese.
People can say what they please.

She says I wasn't born but found.
She's always bossing me around,
She always has to interfere.
Sometimes I wish she'd disappear.

But when it's night and we're in bed
And shadows gather in my head
And I hear whispers everywhere,
It's then I'm glad my sister's there.

I'm dark, she's fair.
She's fire, I'm air.
Two together make a pair.
We're sisters, me and Clare.

Leon Rosselson

Werewolf Granny

When midnight chimes
And the moon is full
And the wind is whistling
Down the hall . . .
When you hear the hoot
Of frightened owls
The werewolf granny prowls

By the light of day
You would never guess
That our dear old granny
In her woolly vest
Sipping her tea
And humming a tune
Will be out in the park
When the night grows dark
Howling at the moon

When midnight chimes
And the moon is full
And the wind is whistling
Down the hall
Lock your door
When you go to bed
Pull the duvet
Over your head
When you hear the hoot
Of frightened owls
The werewolf granny prowls

So be good to your granny
And always say please
Give her a hug,
A kiss and a squeeze
For it might be a rumour
But it just might be true
That one dark dismal night
When the full moon's bright
She will be after you

Roger Stevens

Points of View

My little sister's very shy.
She doesn't speak when spoken to.
She stares at people: doesn't try
to answer – hasn't got a clue.
So I talk FOR her: hope they'll see
it's what SHE'd say, it's not just me.

My brother never lets me talk –
I don't know why – he's nice to me.
But when a grown-up says 'Hello,
and how are you?' they're asking ME,
And then I have to THINK, okay?
But while I'm thinking, he will say
'My sister's all right, aren't you, Sis?'
And so I nod, and smile away –
BUT I WANT TO TELL THEM *MYSELF!*

Constance Boyle

32

Her Auntie's Shoes

She loves to dress up in her auntie's shoes
and click-clack daintily across the floor
over the chequered black and yellow tiles.
She loves to look inside the cupboard door

and find the mirror, like a silver lake
hung up, reflecting beds and floor and her.
She must be careful that she doesn't make
a mess among the folded pillowslips

but scarves . . . her auntie lets her take those
    out.
She puts one round her shoulders like a
    shawl.
Some day she'll be a lady, wearing silk
and dancing at a proper lady's ball.

Her auntie's shoes are cream and brown and
    black.
She'll buy red shoes when she grows up.
    Click-clack.

Adèle Geras

Interesting

I have lots of interests –
my lego, my train set,
my bike, my football.
My hobby is watching my dad
play with them all.

Dave Calder

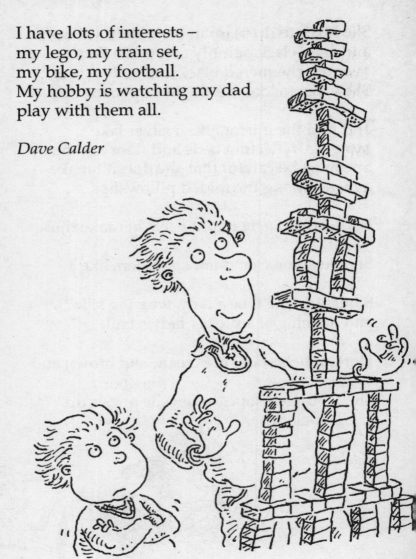

Every Other Sunday

Every other Sunday,
I stand and wait
For Dad to pick me up
Down by the front gate.

If the weather's fine,
We visit the park or zoo.
When it rains, we sit in a cafe
Wondering what to do.

He asks me about school
And what I've done this week.
But everything's different now
And we find it hard to speak.

Every other Sunday,
Dead on half-past four
Dad drops me outside the house,
And waits till I've gone in the door.

John Foster

In the Cellar

The father is sawing, slicing the wood
with strong smooth strokes. The boy
prods a curled shaving with a chisel.

The father is concentrating; his eyes, his
    shoulders, his arms,
are fixed in the wood. The boy is also
    engrossed,
with a sharp corner he has stabbed a jagged
    split.

The father pauses, lays the saw on its side.
    What will he say?
– Now you try, hold it this way –?, or, – does
    that look straight to you –?
No. He says – Stop fiddling. You'll spoil the
    chisel's point.

For what he is teaching is not woodwork, but
    love of making
and patience and care in the work, with the
    tools. And the boy
is learning about his father or perhaps about
    himself

and he puts the chisel back in its place
and he puts his hands in his pockets
and he tries not to lean on the wall.

Dave Calder

Dancing to Mozart

I crept upstairs and pushed the door,
And in the middle of the floor
Grandpa was standing in a trance
Beating the rhythm of a dance.

His eyes were closed, his body swayed,
His toes tapped while the music made
A cloak of glorious, swirling sound
That girdled him and wrapped him round.

He saw me, offered me a hand.
I thought, oh wouldn't it be grand
To dip and circle, lift and sway
With grandpa through the whole long day.

With steps now old and sometimes new
We curtsied, bowed, came close, withdrew;
And while the music swelled and soared
The calls from downstairs were ignored.

Extending arms and bending knees
We danced to MOZART,
If you please.

Gregory Harrison

Brotherly Love

Brother, though I love you dearly
Yet you are a brother, merely
There are times I hate you, really
Could eradicate you, nearly
If I saw you only yearly
I'd adore you, yours sincerely

Paul Bright

Loudspeaker

My Auntie Susan's meek and mild,
And when she comes to call
She whispers in a tiny voice
And makes no sound at all.

But when we're in a busy street
She looks at passers-by
And passes very loud remarks.
(I simply want to die.)

She comments on some woman's hat;
The shape of someone's head;
The rip in someone's tattered jeans.
(My cheeks go burning red.)

She points out someone's bandy legs;
Or someone's broad backside;
Or someone's brightly coloured hair.
(I simply want to hide.)

Oh, when we're on a rush-hour bus
Or somewhere in a crowd,
And everything goes deadly quiet –
WHY MUST SHE TALK SO LOUD!

John Yeoman

Lighthouse

I wanted to go up the lighthouse
on Plymouth Ho.
It was a great tall building
solid and dark against the windy sky.

I can't take you, Mum said,
on account of my claustrophobia.
All those steps; it's too enclosed,
no windows until you reach the top.

I can't take you, Dad said,
on account of my vertigo.
I shall get dizzy and want to jump off.

So they asked a stranger to take me.

We climbed and climbed
until there I stood,
surveying a vast silvery sea,
where the whole world
stretched before me
in a dazzling eternity of colour.

And below me
Mum and Dad
huddled earthbound
like ants, trapped
in a fear they had grown
like the weeds
tangled around the beans
in my dad's garden.

Roger Stevens

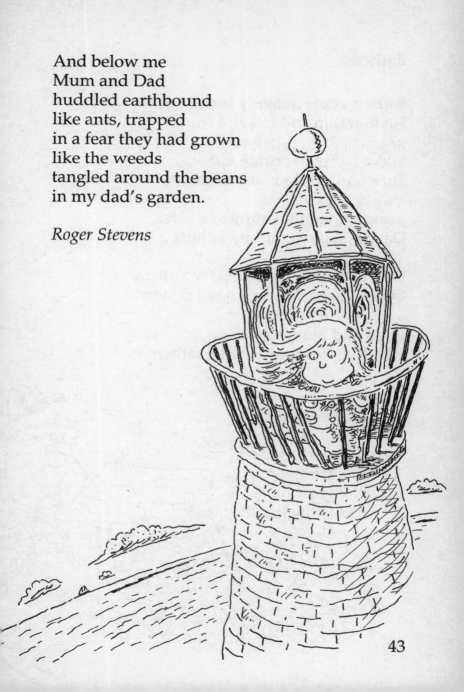

Fathers

Fathers come in every sort:
Fat and thin and tall and short.

Silent fathers, snoring fathers,
Stick 'em up rip roaring fathers.

Jumpy, grumpy, slumpy fathers,
Daring, dandy, dumpy fathers.

Don't be slow and I KNOW fathers,
Quick! Get up and go now! fathers.

D I Y and mowing fathers,
Weeding, reading, sewing fathers,

Swimming, sailing, selling fathers,
Dreamy, story-telling fathers,

Working fathers, shirking fathers,
Once a week and lurking fathers.

Younger, middling, older fathers,
Sit you on their shoulders fathers.

Step fathers, sort-of fathers,
Simple one-and-only fathers,

But whatever fathers be
mine is always mine to me.

Susan Holliday

Twins in the Family

I'm like her
and she's like me.
We both look like each other.

Our Aunt Sue
is a twin too –
she's the image of my mother!

With Uncle Jake
it's like a double-take –
my dad is *his* twin brother!

If we grow up
and we have twins –
we'll be double one another!

John Rice

Brother

I had a little brother
And I brought him to my mother
And I said I want another
Little brother for a change.

But she said don't be a bother
So I took him to my father
And I said this little bother
Of a brother's very strange.

But he said one little brother
Is exactly like another
And every little brother
Misbehaves a bit he said.

So I took the little bother
From my mother and my father
And I put the little bother
Of a brother back to bed.

Mary Ann Hoberman

Great-Grandfather's Watch

This was great-grandfather's watch.
It has a gold face, a gold strap,
a second hand,

a place that tells you the date,
and dashes for numbers,
but I know what they are.

Great-Grandpa was ninety seven,
the oldest person in our family,
the oldest person anyone in my class knew.

He used to sit in a chair,
and shake my hand with his good one,
and say, 'Hello, young man.'

He used to sing 'Gorgonzola Cheese'
and wear a Panama hat indoors,
and give me chocolates.

He won't be there now
when I visit my Leicester Auntie.
I won't see him ever again.

But this was his watch.
He gave it to me,
and it's still ticking.

June Crebbin

I Keep a Photo

I keep a photo of my grandmother.
I have never seen my grandmother.
I keep a photo of her
in my rose box.
My grandmother
sitting on a chair
in the garden.

Sau Yee Kan

The Quarrel

I quarrelled with my brother
I don't know what about,
One thing led to another
And somehow we fell out.
The start of it was slight,
The end of it was strong,
He said he was right,
I knew he was wrong!

We hated one another.
The afternoon turned black.
Then suddenly my brother
Thumped me on the back.
And said, 'Oh, *come* along!
We can't go on all night –
I was in the wrong.'
So he was in the right.

Eleanor Farjeon

Wha Me Mudder Do

Mek me tell you wha me Mudder do
wha me mudder do
wha me mudder do

Me mudder pound plantain mek fufu
Me mudder catch crab mek calaloo stew

Mek me tell you wha me mudder do
wha me mudder do
wha me mudder do

Me mudder beat hammer
Me mudder turn screw
she paint chair red
then she paint it blue

Mek me tell you wha me mudder do
wha me mudder do
wha me mudder do

Me mudder chase bad-cow
with one 'Shoo'
she paddle down river
in she own canoe
Ain't have nothing
dat me mudder can't do
Ain't have nothing
dat me mudder can't do

Mek me tell you

Grace Nichols

Human Affection

Mother, I love you so
Said the child, I love you more than I know.
She laid her head on her mother's arm,
And the love between them kept them warm.

Stevie Smith

Boy in Bubbles

At the family picnic Dad
shook out the tablecloth, Mum
took out the sandwiches, Gran
opened the thermos flask, Uncle
told a rude joke, Cousin
told a ruder one, Uncle
smacked him, Cousin
wailed, Gran
covered her ears, Mum
ate the sandwiches, Dad said

Where's Simon?

A river runs behind the trees
Where the water licks the stones
As the leaves fly out on smoky froth
And the cold bites to the bone

Here, below the blackened weeds,
Beside the bending tree,
Among the crazed and churning foam
A boy dives: he swims, is free

Emma Payne

Sisters

Sally hasn't talked to me for ages.
   She shouts, she swears
   She sneers and jeers, she rages
   She stamps around and slams the door
But doesn't *talk*.
All she'll say to me these days is
'Get lost, go away
Leave me *alone*!'

Sally hasn't laughed with me for ages.
   She doesn't smile
   Or grin or giggle,
   Won't share a joke.
And when I tell her something funny
She throws her eyes up to the ceiling
Says, as if to someone else:
'Why don't that stupid kid shut up.'

Sally hasn't played with me for ages.
   We used to get the doll's house out,
   Go skipping in the street, or
   To the playground in the park together.
But now, it's like it never happened,
She's trying to pretend
Even to me
She's never *played* with anything, not ever.

Sally hasn't wanted me for ages.
    She's getting too *grown-up*
    To be seen with me,
    She reckons.
But I can get my own back, don't you worry.
It's nearly bedtime and I've hidden
The teddy bear
She sleeps with every night.

(And in a little while we'll see
How grown-up my sister Sally
Really is . . .)

Mick Gowar

Family Portrait

When Mrs Hill says
'Paint your family'
I start all right
With Mum and Dad
And Tom and Kim
And Snowy and Patch,
Then my mind fogs up.

I paint Dad out.
For if he's in
Then so is Samantha
His kind-of wife
And their twins.
But none of them live
At our house.

Keith does.
And at weekends
His kids;
It's a squash.
I paint them taking up
A lot of room.

Then I remember the twins
Are my half-brothers.
So I paint Dad back in
With a very small pram
But not Samantha.

I do blobs to get rid of Keith
And I'm just blobbing his kids
When Mrs Hill says 'Oh dear,
That's a bit of a mess.'

Frances Nagle

This is the Mum

This is the mum
Who wakes me up
And gets me out of bed

This is the mum
Who helps me pull
My clean vest over my head

This is the mum
Who irons my clothes
Who puts out my clean socks

This is the mum
Who puts my lunch
Inside my new lunchbox

This is the mum
Who goes to work
Who tries not to be late

This is the mum
Who stands in the rain
By the infant gate

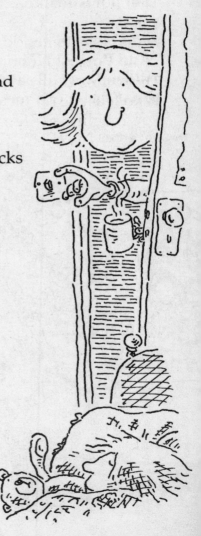

This is the mum
Who later on
Is there to make my tea

This is the mum
Who's looking tired
And occasionally

This is the mum
Who tells me off
For gobbling my food

This is the mum
Who loses her temper
When I'm being rude

This is the mum
Who loves me
At least that's what she said

And this is the mum
Who's telling me
To get myself to bed

Tony Bradman

All Right, Mum?

I do like your dress, Mum,
It's trendy and it's cool,
but I'd wear jeans, if I were you,
to meet me from school.

Can you come in Dad's car?
It's not that yours is bad,
but the stickers in the windows
are a bit sad.

I love the way you've done your hair,
but I should wear a scarf.
No, I don't think it's funny
but my friends might laugh.

Your make-up rather suits you.
You know I'm really glad
my best friend told me yesterday
that I look like my dad.

Of course I'm really proud of you.
I'm not at all ashamed,
and if they ask, 'Whose mother's THAT?'
I can't be blamed.

Celia Warren

Uncle Ben from Number One

Uncle Ben was not a hen
But when he laid an egg
He did it quite professionally
By lifting up a leg.

He studied it and prodded it
And said, 'I'm mystified.'
And then he took it to the kitchen
Where he had it, Fried.

Brian Patten

Acknowledgements

The Publishers gratefully acknowledge the following permission to reproduce copyright material in this book.

'David' from *Strange Goings* On by Diana Hendry, published by Viking 1995; 'Driving at Night with My Dad' copyright © John Rice, 1999. By permission of the author; 'Parentspeak' copyright © Tony Bradman, reprinted by permission of the author; 'Divorce' copyright © Mike Jubb, reprinted by permission of the author; 'Just Mine' copyright © Tony Mitton 1999, reprinted by permission of the author; 'Listening in Bed' copyright © Tony Mitton 1999, reprinted by permission of the author; 'Family Laughs' copyright © Eric Finney, reprinted by permission of the author; 'Sisterly Love' copyright © Judy Waite 1999, reprinted by permission of the author; 'This Week's Bargain Boys' copyright © Judy Waite 1999, reprinted by permission of the author; 'Me' copyright © Tony Bradman, reprinted by permission of the author; 'Walking Home with My Foster Father' by Catherine Benson (first published in *Reflecting Families* by BBC Educational, 1995) by permission of the author; 'Swinging' reprinted by permission of the author, Valerie Bloom; David Higham Associates Ltd for 'Sisters' by Leon Rosselson, copyright © Leon Rosselson 1999; 'Werewolf Granny' reprinted by permission of the author, Roger Stevens; 'Points of View' reprinted by permission of the author, Constance Boyle; 'Her Auntie's Shoes' copyright © Adele Geras 1999. Permission granted by the author; 'Interesting' copyright © Dave Calder 1996, reprinted by permission of the author; 'Every Other Sunday' copyright © John Foster 1995, first published in *Standing on the Sidelines* (Oxford University Press), included by permission of the author; 'In the Cellar' copyright © Dave Calder 1993, reprinted by permission of the author; 'Dancing to Mozart' copyright © Gregory Harrison 1999, reprinted by permission of the author; 'Brotherly Love' copyright © Paul Bright 1999, reprinted by permission of the author; 'Loudspeaker' reprinted by permission of A. P. Watt Ltd on behalf of the author, John Yeoman; 'Lighthouse' reprinted by permission of the author, Roger Stevens; 'Twins in the Family' copyright © John Rice, 1999. By permission of the author; 'Great-Grandfather's Watch' copyright © June Crebbin, reprinted by permission of the author; 'Human Affection' from *The Collected Poems of Stevie Smith*. Reproduced by permission of James MacGibbon; 'Sisters' (pp.10-13, 35 lines) from *Third Time Lucky* by Mick Gowar (Viking Kestrel, 1988) Copyright © Mick Gowar, 1988; 'Family Portrait' from *You can't call a hedgehog Hopscotch* by Frances Nagle, published by Dagger Press 1999; 'This is the Mum' copyright © Tony Bradman, reprinted by permission of the author; 'Uncle Ben from Number One' copyright © Brian Patten 1994. Reproduced by permission of the author c/o Rogers, Coleridge & White Ltd., 20 Powis Mews, London W11 1JN.

Every effort has been made to trace the copyright holders. The publishers would like to hear from any copyright holder not acknowledged.